IMAGES OF ENGLAND

SHEFFIELD
PARKS AND GARDENS

IMAGES OF ENGLAND

SHEFFIELD
PARKS AND GARDENS

DOUGLAS HINDMARCH

TEMPUS

Frontispiece: A wartime picnic. Use of the parks probably reached a peak during the Second World War. In addition to the programme of organised entertainment and activities, people were also encouraged to make more informal use of the parks and open spaces for walking and picnicking. 20,000 copies of a pamphlet giving details of local attractions were distributed free of charge.

First published 2005

Tempus Publishing Limited
The Mill, Brimscombe Port,
Stroud, Gloucestershire, GL5 2QG
www.tempus-publishing.com

© Douglas Hindmarch, 2005

The right of Douglas Hindmarch to be identified as the Author
of this work has been asserted in accordance with the
Copyrights, Designs and Patents Act 1988.

British Library Cataloguing in Publication Data.
A catalogue record for this book is available from the British Library.

ISBN 0 7524 3542 6

Typesetting and origination by Tempus Publishing Limited.
Printed in Great Britain.

Contents

Acknowledgements

Most of the photographs and other illustrations in this book are from Sheffield Libraries' Local Studies Library. It is sometimes difficult to identify individual contributors to the collections and inevitably some will have passed away and others will have been forgotten. With apologies to those who may have been omitted, I would like to thank the following who in the past have donated or lent photographs which have been included in the book: J.M. Ambler, Mr(s) Andrews, S.B. Atkinson, R. Barrett, A.W. Bourne, D.H. Colver, K.F. Coupe, Mrs Dean, Mrs M. Edwards, J. Farnon, F. Goodliffe, Mrs Gurney, Miss Hemmingfield, Mrs P. Higgins, C. Hill, K. Howard, C.H. Lea, Mrs V. Lloyd, G.E. Saville, R.S. Smith, Miss C. Traunter, Mrs E. Wilmot.

Much credit is due to the library staff who over the years have organised, catalogued and cared for the photographs. The last few years have brought major changes with the launch of *Picture Sheffield,* a computer system which has made the collections more accessible and has also been of enormous help in selecting the photographs. Mike Spick, Michelle Hall and Mary Rhodes have been largely responsible for its development. Thanks also to Mike and Michelle for their help in preparing the images and to all the staff in Local Studies for their support and encouragement during the preparation of the book.

I am grateful to Janice Maskort, the City Librarian, for permission to reproduce the photographs from Sheffield Libraries' collections, to Sarah Barber and Ian Mitchell of Sheffield City Council's Parks, Woodlands and Countryside Service for their help and the loan of photographs and to Sheffield Newspapers for permission to use the photographs on pages 122 (bottom) and 126. Also, Joan Sewell whose research into the history of Sheffield's parks has been the source for some of the background information.

Finally, I would like to thank my daughter Sarah for her helpful suggestions. She is a brass band player herself, but will take pleasure in reminding me of the comments of the Parks and Burial Grounds Committee at the foot of page 59.

Introduction

Sheffield is justifiably proud of the parks, woodlands and open spaces which make it one of the greenest cities in Europe. It has not always been the case. By the early nineteenth century the rapid expansion of the town had brought appalling living conditions, overcrowding and poverty and, as James Smith observed in his *Report on the conditions of the Town of Sheffield* for the Royal Commission on Health of Towns in 1842, 'There are no public gardens or open space of any extent for the people to walk and enjoy themselves in'. By this time the need to provide adequate space for recreation in urban areas had been recognised but the only provision in Sheffield was the Botanical Gardens, owned by a private company and open only to subscribers except on a few days each year.

In 1841 the Duke of Norfolk proposed laying out part of the former Sheffield Park to provide recreational space for the working classes. Norfolk Park opened in 1848 and although it remained in private ownership until 1909, the public was allowed access at all times. It was one of the earliest public parks in the country.

The involvement of local authorities began with the 1860 Public Improvements Act which permitted the levy of a rate to pay for the maintenance of open spaces. The Weston Hall estate was purchased in 1873 and Weston Park became Sheffield's first municipal park. The creation of parks was a matter of great civic pride and in 1897 the City Council's General Purposes and Parks Committee recorded its achievements in a book, *Plans and Descriptions of Parks and Recreation Grounds*. It detailed six major parks, created mainly from the grounds of former private houses and in some cases lying outside the existing boundaries. The problem of providing open spaces nearer to the heavily built-up areas was partly addressed by the creation of a number of smaller, less formal recreation grounds. The Committee had also acquired part of Whiteley Woods and, along with the Rivelin estate owned by the Water Committee, this brought into public ownership some of the attractive surrounding areas which were already recognised as one of the distinctive features of Sheffield.

Parks and woodlands continued to be acquired through donation and purchase. They included Great Roe Wood (1898), Abbeyfield (1909), Millhouses (1909) and Hutcliffe Wood (1911). In 1911 Loxley Chase was given to the city, 'to be maintained forever for the enjoyment of the public and to keep its rural character'. This period also saw the further development of sports and recreational facilities. Sports pitches, boating lakes and refreshment pavilions had already been provided in some parks but these were supplemented by bowling greens and tennis courts, Sheffield's first municipal golf course and a bathing pool in the Rivelin Valley. Music had also become a popular attraction and in 1899 permanent bandstands were provided in the major parks.

In 1919 Professor Patrick Abercrombie was appointed to prepare a development plan for the city. His report, published in 1924, called for a doubling of the acreage of open spaces which Sheffield then possessed. He also highlighted the need for children's playgrounds in the central area, the special character of the 'Porter Brook Parkway' and the value of maintaining public access to the surrounding moorlands. The report was apparently never officially adopted but some of the proposals were put into effect, thanks largely to the generosity of J.G. Graves. His gifts led to the opening of Graves and Concord Parks, the construction of playgrounds, the completion of Sheffield's famous Round Walk and the protection of important open spaces such as Ecclesall Woods and Blacka Moor.

During the Second World War the Parks Department was active in promoting food production and in organising activities in the parks. Sheffield's Holidays at Home programme, intended to encourage people to spend leisure time close to home, was one of the most successful in the country. It was estimated that use of the parks had doubled during the war and there was a feeling of optimism for the post-war years.

Whirlow Brook Park opened in 1946 and a number of schemes were completed to mark the 1951 Festival of Britain. To attract visitors to the parks, the most successful parts of the wartime entertainment programme were retained and the Food Production Show became the Sheffield Show. However, there were also some losses. Part of Weston Park made way for new university buildings and declining attendances led to the end of the seasons of band concerts in 1957. In 1958 the City Council approved the demolition of the bandstands in Hillsborough, Meersbrook and Endcliffe Parks.

Changes in the use of leisure time and greater mobility meant that fewer people were now visiting parks. The financial difficulties of the City Council during the 1980s and 1990s also resulted in reduced maintenance and security, the loss of amenities through vandalism and neglect and little encouragement for people to make use of the open spaces. However, in recent years there has been some change in fortunes and greater local and national recognition of the importance of parks and recreational areas. The historic parks such as the Botanical Gardens and Norfolk Park have attracted grants for restoration work while renewed commitment and investment by the City Council has helped to reverse the decline. Voluntary groups have also been active and now play a key role in the management and maintenance of some parks. These partnerships between the City Council and the various community groups and other organisations should help to ensure that the people of Sheffield can continue to enjoy their green heritage.

Although the chapters follow the same chronological arrangement as this brief historical introduction, this compilation is not intended to be an illustrated history of Sheffield's parks. However, I hope that the photographs show some of the interesting features of the parks, many of them now gone, and illustrate how they have had an important role in the life of the city. The pictures may also revive some happy memories and encourage an interest in both the history and the future of these parks, cemeteries, woodlands and open spaces. Inevitably the selection of images has been dictated by the limitations of space and by the availability of good-quality photographs. The emphasis is almost entirely on areas now owned by the City Council. There are also sometimes unexplained gaps in the photographic record but I hope that there will be some images that are new to those who enjoy books of old photographs. Most frustrating of all is the knowledge that many photographs have been lost. However, it is always surprising what does survive and if anyone has photographs they think would be of interest, please contact the Local Studies Library in the Central Library. A wider selection of photographs of Sheffield is also available in Local Studies or on the website at *www.picturesheffield.com*

one

The First Parks

GRAND OPENING

OF THE

Sheffield Botanical and Horticultural Gardens,

TO THE

PROPRIETORS AND THE PUBLIC,

UNDER THE PATRONAGE OF

HIS GRACE THE DUKE OF NORFOLK,
HIS GRACE THE DUKE OF DEVONSHIRE,
THE RIGHT HONOURABLE EARL FITZWILLIAM,
THE RIGHT HONOURABLE LORD WHARNCLIFFE,
THE RIGHT HONOURABLE THE EARL OF SURREY,
THE HONOURABLE J. S. WORTLEY.

ON WEDNESDAY and THURSDAY, the 29th and 30th Days of June Instant. Tickets of Admission, TWO SHILLINGS EACH, and Children under Fourteen Years of Age at One Shilling each, may be had at any of the Newspaper Offices, and at the Two Entrance Lodges.

And on MONDAY and TUESDAY, the 4th and 5th Days of July, the Garden will be opened at ONE SHILLING each, and Children under Fourteen Years of Age at Sixpence each, from the hour of ELEVEN in the Forenoon to NINE o'Clock in the Evening. Admission Tickets, for the Two Last Days, to be had at the Entrance Lodges only.

The Committee will spare no Expence in making the Fete on the opening of these Extensive Gardens and Pleasure Grounds most attractive; and, although the Grounds are not completely finished, yet their present advanced state of beauty, together with the variety of architectural magnificence in the surrounding picturesque Scenery, cannot fail to strike the Visitor with delight.

Two Bands of Music (the Cavalry and an Auxiliary), will be in constant attendance to enliven the gaity of the days. A variety of Refreshments of the very best kind will be provided at moderate charges.

☞ Coaches will be stationed at the Old Church Gates, at Eleven o'Clock in the Morning, to convey Visitors to the Garden at Sixpence each.

The opening of the Botanical Gardens is announced in the Sheffield Mercury on 25 June 1836. Although the entrance fees were 2s for the first two days and 1s for the other days, substantial sums at the time, it was reported that over 12,000 people attended.

Botanical Gardens, Sheffield

An engraving of the new Botanical Gardens. The Sheffield Botanical and Horticultural Society was formed in June 1833 following a meeting called by Thomas Dunn, the Master Cutler, and 18 acres of land were bought from the Wilson family of Sharrow in 1834 for £3,600. The competition to design the gardens was won by Robert Marnock, the gardener at Bretton Hall, Wakefield, and he was appointed the first Curator. Marnock later became the Curator of the Royal Botanic Society at Regent's Park and his other work in Sheffield included Weston Park, the grounds of High Hazels and the gardens at Kenwood for George Wostenholm.

The Botanical Gardens are perhaps best known for the conservatories, sometimes known locally as the Paxton Pavilions. They were designed by the Sheffield architect Benjamin Broomhead Taylor, who was also responsible for the main entrance on Clarkehouse Road. The three main pavilions, each with a quadrangular glass dome, were linked by lower glazed colonnades. The photograph, possibly taken in about 1890, also shows the glasshouses at each end of the range which were added in the 1850s.

The interior of one of the linking colonnades. The imported plants on display in the conservatories were a great attraction for visitors. The Central Pavilion was originally a tropical palm house while the others housed temperate plants. Perhaps the most famous specimen to be seen was the Victoria Regia water lily. Its leaves grew to 6-12ft in diameter and on one occasion a leaf is said to have supported the weight of the Curator sitting on a chair.

BOTANICAL GARDENS

C. GRAY. Sc.

B. B. Taylor, Sheffield, Architect.

SHEFFIELD BOTANICAL GARDENS.

Another element of the design was the creation of smaller areas with rock gardens, pools and landscape features which could be explored along winding paths. The sender of this card explained that, 'This part of the Gardens used to be an old pond but it went dry so it was planted out in beds of flowers. It's busier than this on Sundays.'

Opposite, above: Some of the formal planting in the Botanical Gardens and a view across the lawns. The gardens were originally laid out in the Gardenesque style and, although this postcard dates from the 1900s when some alterations had been made to the layout, it is still possible to see the way in which trees and shrubs were planted in an informal natural setting while formal beds and borders provided a display of colour.

Opposite, below: This engraving of the fountain and the wide promenade path leading to the Central Pavilion appeared in the first volume of the *Floricultural Magazine* in 1836, together with a description of the newly opened gardens. The magazine was edited by Marnock and published in Sheffield by Ridge and Jackson. It was one of the leading horticultural journals of the time.

Botanical Gardens. Sheffield

This must have been the scene on a typical Sunday that the correspondent on the previous page had in mind. The original card is an example of an early divided-back postcard which allowed a message to be written on the back as well as in the space below the picture. They were introduced in 1902. The card was published by the well-known Sheffield department store, John Walsh Ltd.

Left: The Botanical and Horticultural Society arranged a number of gala days each year to attract visitors and one of the most popular events was the Band of Hope Gala. The Band of Hope was a temperance organisation which arranged an educational programme, particularly for children. Its members took the 'pledge': 'I promise to abstain from all intoxicating liquors, from tobacco, snuff, and gambling, and as far as possible to discountenance their use and practice.'

Opposite, below: A wagon decorated by John Street Band of Hope. Gala Day began with a procession of bands and decorated wagons from the fairground to the Botanical Gardens. At the gardens the visitors were entertained by massed choirs of children and by other displays and exhibitions. The children were required to attend at least seven rehearsals before the gala and their reward on the day was a mug of tea and a piece of plum loaf for 3d, provided by the organising committee. Inevitably there was only tea and ginger beer for other visitors.

14

Promenade concerts were another popular attraction, as this picture taken in around 1895 shows. Some of the visitors can be seen seated in front of the Central Pavilion while others 'promenade' to the music of the band. As one writer in the *Sheffield Telegraph* recalled, 'the ladies dressed in their best, promenaded, chatted, and flirted to the music of a band. Marriages may be made in heaven, but a number of Sheffield marriages were hatched at the 'Proms'.'

The entrance to the bear pit in the early 1900s when it was showing some obvious signs of neglect. This was an original feature of the gardens but there is some doubt about its exact use. The bears may have been there until about 1870 when, according to a later letter in the local newspaper, there was an unfortunate accident in which a nurse held a child over the railings to see the bears and the child was clawed to death. It has not been possible to verify this story.

One of the shelters, c.1895. This probably stood on Birch Hill, the highest point in the gardens, which commanded fine views of the main lawn and pavilions. There was also a separate glazed pavilion in another area which was used for exhibitions and as a refreshment room on gala days. This was probably the tearoom which in 1899 was reported to have been demolished following the takeover by the Town Trustees.

A lady poses for a casual photograph on one of the seats by the bandstand, probably on a cold day in about 1900. The Ordnance Survey map shows that there was a bandstand on this site in front of the Central Pavilion by 1889, but there may have been a temporary structure before this permanent building.

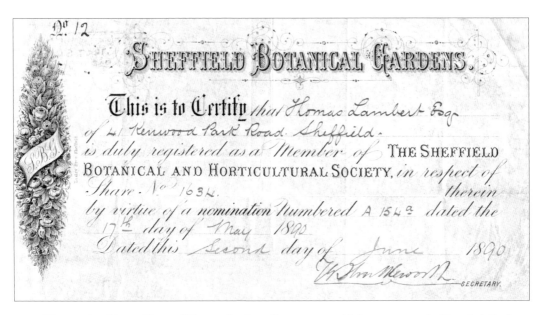

The membership certificate of Thomas Lambert. Except on special days, access to the Botanical Gardens was restricted to shareholders. After expenditure of £18,000 the original Sheffield Botanical and Horticultural Society found itself in financial difficulties and in 1844 it was sold to a new company for £9,000, raised in £5 shares. Shareholders paid an annual subscription of 12s 6d (later raised to 15s) which entitled the bearer and his family to admittance to the gardens. In the 1890s the society was again in difficulties and in 1898 the Sheffield Town Trust took over the management.

Above: One of the attendants near the main entrance, probably in around 1905. When the Town Trust assumed control the gardens were opened to the public. One of the duties of the attendants would have been to enforce the byelaws approved by the trustees. One of these stated, 'No person of notoriously bad character shall enter... nor any person in a state of intoxication, or suffering from any contagious infection or loathsome disease, or so dirty in clothes or person as to be an annoyance to the public.' The main entrance and the Curator's house can be seen in the background.

Above: In May 1962 an aviary was opened in the Central Pavilion. The various cages or flights housed over 300 foreign birds including budgerigars, parrots, cockatoos and finches. In 1964 an aquarium was also constructed in the West Pavilion. The aviary was closed in 1991 during an outbreak of disease among the birds and a decision was subsequently taken to permanently close both the aviary and the aquarium.

Right: One of the most popular attractions was the macaws, which could often be seen outside the aviary. It was home to a large red and blue macaw named Sir Mortimer Wheeler and a blue and gold bird called Poppet, who had a habit of grabbing buttons off visitors' coats.

Opposite, below: The parasols are out and the gardens look their very best on this summer day. In October 1902 the *Sheffield Independent* published drawings of proposed alterations to the gardens which involved the demolition of the colonnades between the pavilions. Postmarks on some of the postcards indicate that they had gone by 1905. They have been reinstated as part of the recent restoration work. The large cast-iron urns which line the path were part of a set of twelve designed for the gardens in 1836. Ten of the urns were stolen on the night of 28 May 1969 but fortunately they were recovered by the police.

The seating installed around the Crimea Monument provided a welcome resting place for these ladies in August 1961. The monument originally stood at Moorhead, the foundation stone having been laid by the Duke of Cambridge on 21 October 1857. In 1959 road improvements were planned and the figure of Victory was removed from its tall column and re-erected on part of the base in the Botanical Gardens. Parts of the granite column found a use in a children's playground. The site chosen for the monument had originally been occupied by the fountain and in 2004, as part of the scheme to restore the gardens to their original design, it was removed and the fountain reinstated. It is now in storage until a new site is found.

Right: Some of the 10,000 panes of glass in the roof of the Central Pavilion in 1956. In December 1951 the gardens were transferred to Sheffield Corporation on a ninety-nine year lease at a rent of 1s per year. One of the major tasks facing the Parks Department was the restoration of the pavilions, which had been damaged during the war. This was, in fact, the second disaster to hit the conservatories. On 5 July 1843 a freak hailstorm had broken 5,700 square yards of glass.

Below: The West Pavilion during restoration in 1957. The work was undertaken by a local firm, Mellowes & Co., who were able to replace the ribs using an iron which closely matched the original material. Repairs to the other pavilions followed in 1958.

An engraving by T.C. Hofland which was commissioned to promote the new General Cemetery. In 1834 the first meeting of subscribers to the General Cemetery Company was held at Cutlers Hall. The formation of the company was a response by predominantly Nonconformist members of the new middle class to the inadequate provision for burials in the town. The 9 acres of land by the River Porter bought for £1,900 provided an ideal site and Samuel Worth won a competition for the design of the cemetery. As White's 1837 *History and General Directory of Sheffield* reported, 'It is indisputably one of the most beautiful establishments of the kind in the kingdom; and though some of its chief attractions are attributable to the situation, it is much indebted to the skill and taste of the architect Mr Worth, who has made it a delightful spot for the perambulation of the living, and a safe depository for the dead.' The first burial, that of twenty-four year old Mary Ann Fish, who had died of consumption, took place on 26 May 1836. The engraving shows a hearse, preceded by two mutes on foot, approaching the gatehouse which was built over the River Porter. The catacombs, which never proved to be popular, curve around the hillside and above them are the chapel and the company's offices.

Right: A list of the charges at the General Cemetery in 1844. The cemetery had not been as popular as expected and by this time the original fees had been reduced in an attempt to attract more business. A single grave now cost from £1 15s 0d, depending on situation, and a private vault from £5 5s 0d. The company was also increasingly reliant on the income from pauper burials, paid for by the Guardians. One pauper's grave in the General Cemetery has ninety-six internments in a single plot.

Below: Two obelisks stood at the side of the turnpike to mark the entrance to the tree-lined avenue leading to the gatehouse. They remained in place as houses spread along the appropriately named Cemetery Avenue. The photograph probably dates from around 1903 when, as the building plot surrounded by advertising hoardings shows, development of this part of Ecclesall Road was not quite complete.

CHARGES

AT THE

SHEFFIELD GENERAL CEMETERY.

	£.	s.	D.
A single Interment – Children under six years of age	0	4	6
Do. do. from six years and upwards	0	6	0
A single Interment, with an inscription of name, age, and time of decease, on stone	1	0	0
Interment of a still born Child	0	1	0
Land for a private Grave, varying in £1. 15s. 0d. price according to situation .... and upwards.			
For sinking the same nine feet, including all expenses of the first Interment	0	17	6
For each future Interment therein	0	14	6
An extra charge will be made for depths below nine feet.			
A private Vault, or Crypt, for a single Interment....	5	5	0
A Family Vault, varying according to £12. 12s. 0d. size and situation .... and upwards.			
For the first Interment in a Vault................. ..	0	14	6
For each subsequent Int rment therein	1	2	0
Extra charges for Interments before One o'Clock in the Day	0	10	6

NO ADDITIONAL CHARGE WILL BE MADE FOR FEES.

The parties attending any Interment, may avail themselves of the services of the Chaplain of the Institution, or of their own Minister, and use what Form of Service they may prefer.

GRAVE and VAULT STONES are furnished by the Directors, at moderate charges.

The Deed of Settlement being enrolled in Chancery, this Cemetery can never be appropriated to any other purpose.

Innocent, Printer.

The Anglican chapel in December 1940, showing some of the damage caused during the Sheffield Blitz. In 1850 a new consecrated section was added to the cemetery to try to meet the demands of the established church and, also, to safeguard the business of pauper burials. New legislation required these to be in consecrated ground. Robert Marnock, by then a well-known landscape architect, planned the extension and the new Anglican chapel, whose spire dominates the area, was designed by William Flockton.

James Montgomery, the famous poet and editor of the *Sheffield Iris*, died on 30 April 1854 and was buried in front of the Anglican chapel. The monument, sculpted by John Bell but said to be a poor likeness, was erected by public subscription in 1861. In 1971 his body was exhumed and placed in a new vault in the cathedral forecourt. The monument was placed over the vault and rededicated at a service on 17 June 1971.

The memorial to Mark Firth, leading industrialist and former Lord Mayor and Master Cutler, who died in 1880. The granite memorial is topped by a draped urn and surrounded by elaborate railings made in Firth's Norfolk Works. The memorial has recently been restored with the help of funding provided by the University of Sheffield as part of its centenary celebrations in 2005. Other prominent local people buried in the cemetery include the Cole brothers, George Bassett (who founded the confectionery firm), and Samuel Holberry, a leading figure in the Chartist movement whose funeral was attended by 50,000 people.

Part of the General Cemetery in 1978. After the Second World War the cemetery became much neglected as the company's income declined and maintenance costs increased. Proposals included development of the site for housing but it was acquired by the City Council and closed by an Act of Parliament. By this time there had been about 86,350 burials. This consecrated section was cleared to create a new open space.

Above: On 8 July 1832 cholera struck Sheffield. By the time the last case was reported on 27 October the disease had struck 1,347 people, of whom 402 died. The early victims were interred in the churchyards of St Philip's and St George's but as the epidemic became more serious the Duke of Norfolk provided a site at Sheffield Park for mass burials; 339 bodies were eventually buried there. The only marked grave is that of John Blake, the Master Cutler, but funds were raised for a public memorial. The Cholera Monument was designed by M.E. Hadfield and the foundation stone laid on 10 December 1834, when a record of the epidemic was placed under the stone. The Monument Grounds remained in the ownership of the Duke and it had been closed for a number of years when, in 1899, the City Council negotiated a twenty-one year lease at a nominal rent of 2s per year. The monument was subsequently repaired, railings erected and paths laid. The photograph dates from this period. The paths, steps and seats appear to be new and the repairs to the stonework are clearly visible. The lease was later renewed and the grounds eventually passed into public ownership in perpetuity. In 1990 the monument was badly damaged in a storm and for a time only a stump remained. Restoration work was completed in 2004 and the memorial rededicated by the Duke of Norfolk on 26 May.

Opposite, above: An engraving of Norfolk Park with the town beyond, dated 23 February 1860. The Duke of Norfolk's intention to create a park was made public in 1841 when his agent, Mr Michael Ellison, declined to make a donation to the Botanical Gardens on the grounds that it was not accessible to members of the 'working classes'. He suggested that the Duke would 'more effectively promote the health and enjoyment of the most numerous portion of the inhabitants of Sheffield by planting and forming into a park 40 or 50 acres of ground within a reasonable distance of the town and throwing the same open to the public'.

Opposite, below: The Granville Road entrance to Norfolk Park, *c.*1910. The lodge dates from 1851 but at that time the approach from the town would have been along Norfolk Road. Granville Road was not completed until around 1880.

Norfolk Park, Sheffield

NORFOLK PARK ENTRANCE FROM INSIDE. SHEFFIELD   G.B & SONS Nº 151.

Norfolk Park is a hive of activity as final preparations are made for the arrival of Queen Victoria on 21 May 1897 to attend the Duke of Norfolk's Invitation Gathering of Children. Workmen are ensuring that the Royal Standard can be unfurled at the appropriate moment and the conductor's platform is ready for Dr Henry Coward to take his place. Further up the hill the collection point for lost children is likely to have a busy day.

This general view of the park being prepared for the royal visit shows the newly constructed Queen's Drive. In 1959 the valley was filled in to create the level events arena, most of the material coming from slum clearance in the park district.

It would prove to be a long day for those lucky enough to receive a ticket. For the children it meant a walk or a wagon or tram ride to marshalling centres at Queen's Road, Cambridge Street, Bank Street, Nursery Street, Carlisle Street, Effingham Road or Intake Road and a further march to the park. The Queen herself was due to arrive in procession from the Town Hall at 6.10 p.m. and, after the singing of the National Anthem, two verses of a song written especially for the occasion and *Rule Britannia*, she was scheduled to leave at 6.20 p.m.

⊶⊷ THE DUKE OF NORFOLK'S ⊷⊶

Invitation Gathering of Children in Norfolk Park, Sheffield, to welcome Her Majesty the Queen, 21st May, 1897.

CARD OF ADMISSION
To Reserved Enclosure. J

[NOTE. The enclosure is to the right of the Upper Carriage Drive leading from the Main Entrance in Norfolk Road, near to the Booth marked "Police"].

☞ **Please be in your place by 4 o'clock.**

The Queen's carriage can hardly be seen among the massed ranks of over 40,000 children. In the background are some of the refreshment booths where, after Her Majesty's departure, the children could exchange their tickets for a bun and a drink. One of the newspapers described the catering arrangements. 'All the children passed in one way and out by the other into an open space, where large wooden erections, like glorified sheep troughs, full of lemon juice and milk and water, enabled the children to get their mugs filled with commendable speed.' Children also received a commemorative medal from the Duke of Norfolk.

The entrance to Norfolk Park in about 1905, this time from Granville Road. The gateway and flanking walls were built in 1876 to designs by M.E. Hadfield & Son and the crest and motto of the Dukes of Norfolk was displayed over the gate. The magnificent lamp with five lanterns originally stood at the junction of Queen's Road and Granville Road but it was moved in the early 1900s as traffic increased.

The gates of Norfolk Park seem to have been a popular location for official photographs. These Daimler buses outside the Norfolk Park Road entrance were among the first motor vehicles operated by Sheffield Corporation Tramways when bus services began in 1913.

The avenue of lime trees leading from the Norfolk Park Road entrance was one of the outstanding features of the original design of Norfolk Park. The notice on the gatepost prohibiting motorcars and cycles is signed Henry Coverdale, Norfolk Estate Office. This indicates that the photograph was probably taken before 1909, when the Duke of Norfolk presented the park to the city.

The only words which can be read on the poster by the entrance to Norfolk Park are 'Wild birds'. Is feeding the birds on this wintry day to be approved of or discouraged? The lodge, gateway and screen wall are contemporary with the opening of the park.

Above: In 1912 the Sheffield Sunday School Union celebrated its centenary and Norfolk Park held the principal Whitsuntide gathering in the city. Nearly 12,000 pupils, teachers and supporters from forty-one schools assembled in the park and the *Sheffield Independent* described the scene. 'Bounded by a line of brightly coloured banners with trees as a background, the gathering made a very striking picture for a crowd of about 8,000 people on the rising ground immediately opposite. The singing, energetically conducted by Mr Lawrence Chadwick and led by a band for which Mr H. Revitt was responsible, went remarkably well.' Perhaps the arrangements did not always run so smoothly.

Left: After the formal proceedings the Sunday schools dispersed and returned to their own churches where a special tea would often be provided.

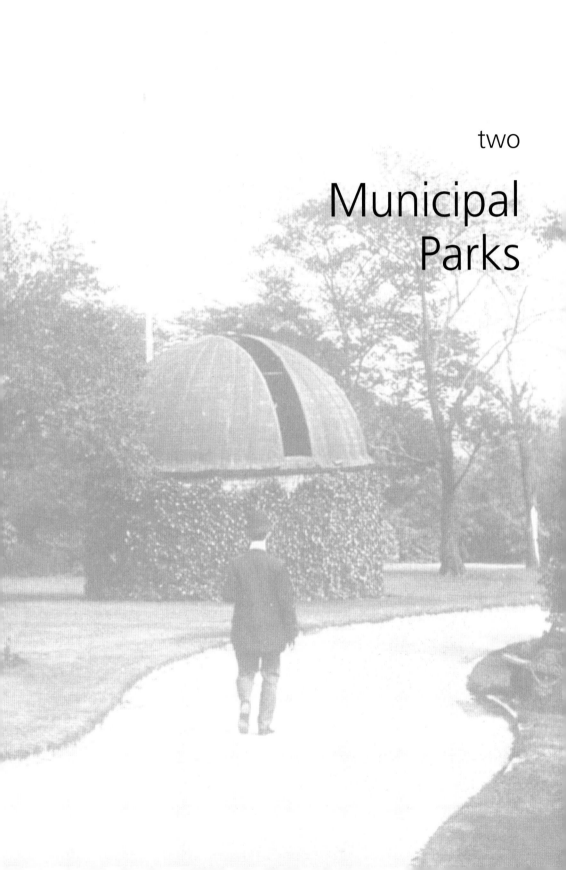

two

Municipal Parks

1169. FROZEN FOUNTAIN, WESTON PARK, SHEFFIELD.

Above: Weston Park Museum and the gardens. Weston Hall was built for Thomas Harrison, who died in 1818. Following the death of his wife in 1823, his daughters Anne and Eliza inherited the house and it remained the family home until 1873 when Eliza died. The 12½ acre estate was then purchased by the Town Council for £18,000. Sheffield's first public park opened to visitors on 4 May 1874 but at that time both the house and the grounds were largely unaltered. Robert Marnock was asked to design the new park and plans were also made to convert the house for use as a museum. The museum opened on 6 September 1875.

Left: The ice formations on the Weston Park fountain must have been an attraction during severe winters. A number of different postcards were published but this example produced by Robert Sneath is not dated. A very similar postcard published by J.W. Mottershaw gives the date 17 January 1905.

The Observatory was rebuilt in Weston Park to house a large telescope originally owned by Thomas Rawson Barker and presented to the town by his daughter. It opened on 20 September 1880 and the Curator of the museum was available on Wednesday and Saturday evenings during the winter months to give instruction and to supervise visitors. It is believed to have been removed during the Second World War.

Inside the Observatory. For the technically minded, the telescope was equatorially mounted, was 8ft in diameter focal length, had an object lens 6in in diameter and had nine eyepieces of various powers. It was also fitted with a clockwork drive to keep it fixed on an object. This was particularly useful when visitors were waiting their turn to observe the night sky.

Part of the brief message on the back of this card, posted on 1 March 1906, tells the recipient that 'The place on the other side is the Mappin Art Gallery'. John Newton Mappin left £15,000 in his will for the art gallery, as well as 153 paintings to form the basis of the collection. It was opened on 27 July 1887.

The Weston Park gardeners and one of the uniformed park keepers. The gentleman on the left is said to be John Swallow. In *White's General and Commercial Directory of Sheffield* for 1898 he is described as a 'jobbing gardener' so perhaps he also helped to maintain the private gardens of well-off Sheffielders.

Rehearsals taking place in Weston Park in preparation for the visit of King Edward VII and Queen Alexandra in 1905. The main purpose of the royal visit was to open the new University of Sheffield, but the King also presented new Colours to the 2nd Battalion, King's Own Yorkshire Light Infantry. Here the soldiers, in khaki service dress, have an opportunity to relax while their officers discuss some of the arrangements.

On 12 July the men of the King's Own Yorkshire Light Infantry, now in full dress uniform, are drawn up to receive His Majesty. Privileged guests have a close view of the proceedings while other spectators line the roof of the museum and the Mappin Art Gallery to catch a glimpse of the King and Queen. Afterwards there was a garden party and tea was served in a marquee in the park.

Above: These visitors seem to be admiring the lake in Weston Park but in 1874 it had been described as a 'pond which is now anything but attractive in its character'. It was enlarged and improved as part of the development of the park and the fountain is just visible beyond the baby in the bassinet. The photograph was probably taken soon after the opening of the university in 1905.

Left: The lake could be crossed at two points by rustic bridges, a style of construction which seems to have been adopted for most of the parks at this time. One of the lake's ducks is also in the picture. The wildfowl were carefully documented in Committee minutes and this could be one of the descendants of the two ducks and a drake which were presented to Weston Park by the Bandon Duck Company of Ireland in 1888.

Opposite, below: Members of the Police Band have left their music stands while they pose for the photograph. Just visible inside the bandstand are some lamps. In 1913 it was reported that the bandstands had been illuminated for evening concerts.

Weston Park, Sheffield. No. 1545.

Above: The lawns and bandstand in Weston Park. The Observatory is just visible on the left. Concerts became a popular attraction and performances were given by local bands with long-forgotten names such as Grimesthorpe Wesleyan Reform, Dannemora, Sheffield Temperance, Hardy Patent Pick Company, Perseverance Brass and Reed, Oak Street Orchestral and Walkley St Mary's. The bandstand was one of five ordered by the General Purposes and Parks Committee in 1899.

CITY OF   SHEFFIELD.

Music in the Parks and Open Spaces.

SEASON 1914.

Chairman of Bands Sub-Committee: Coun. JOSEPH KAYE.   Organiser: ARTHUR S. BURROWS.

Weston Park, Monday, July 13th, 1914.

Band of H.M. Scots Guards

By kind permission of COLONEL F. J. HEYWORTH, D.S.O.

Bandmaster - - - - - Mr. FRED W. WOOD.

EVENING, 7-30 to 9-30 p.m.

1	MARCH	"The Spirit of Pageantry"	*Fletcher*
2	OVERTURE	"Morning, Noon, and Night"	*Suppé*

Franz Von Suppé who was a nephew of Donizetti, sprang from a family of Belgian origin. He was born in 1820 at Spalato, in Dalmatia, and, while still a child, began to compose little pieces for the flute, on which he had already learned to play. On the death of his father, his mother removed to Vienna, and her son became a student at the Conservatoire there—his progress being so rapid that, while still in his teens, he was appointed conductor at the Josephstadt Theatre. He officiated in this capacity at various Theatres for over 30 years. As a composer Suppé was gifted in unusual degree. To astonishing fecundity he united a pleasant vein of melody and thoroughly sound musical instincts. He produced two grand operas, over a hundred and fifty comic operas, vaudevilles, and musical farces, and also wrote a mass, a symphony, some quartets, and a requiem. Only two of his operas have been produced in England, namely, "Fatinitza," and "Boccaccio." Suppé died at Vienna in May, 1895.

3	VALSE	"The Fairest in the Land"	*Ancliffe*
4	SELECTION	"Merrie England"	*German*
5	INTERMEZZO	"In the Night"	*Gilbert*
6	UNGARISCHE RHAPSODIE, No. 1		*Liszt*

Liszt's Hungarian Rhapsodies (of which he wrote fifteen), reproduce with great fidelity, but in an idealised form, the strong contrasts of expression, rhythm, speed and the brilliant and lavish ornamentation that characterise the performances in Hungary of national music by gypsy bands. One of the most famous of these bands, directed by a violinist named Bihary, was engaged by the Emperor of Austria to entertain the numerous distinguished guests who met at the Congress in Vienna in 1813-15, and so astonished and delighted them that during the next few years gipsy bands became quite the rage of the various capitals of Europe. It was during one of Bihary's tours that Liszt (then but a boy) heard him play. That the effect was powerful and lasting we have direct evidence from the vivid description of Bihary's playing and personal characteristics in Liszt's delightful book, "Des Bohemiens et de leur Musique en Hongrie," written in 1859, thirty-two years after Bihary's death. It was this style of playing that Liszt took as his model, when, many years later, he enshrined the melodies of his native land in the series of Rhapsodies which have since become so famous.

7	SELECTION	"Romeo and Juliet"	*Gounod*

Charles Gounod (1818-1893), composer and organist, born and died in Paris. Studied at the Paris Conservatoire, where he obtained the first prize for composition. Spent some time in Rome, Vienna, and in England. Up to 1851 he had composed many excellent works, and it was in this year that "Faust" was performed for the first time and met with a tremendous success. "Faust" established Gounod's reputation, and was followed by "La Colombe," "La Reine de Saba," "Mireille," and "Romeo et Juliet," the latter of which is considered even finer than his "Faust."

8	(a) INTERMEZZO	"Laughing Eyes"	*Finck*
	(b) HUMORESKE	"Kilties Kourtship"	*Mackenzie*
9	BALLET EGYPTIENNE		*Luigini*
10	XYLOPHONE SOLO	"The Orchid"	*W. Underhill*
		Soloist, CORPORAL MORGAN.	late Scots Guards.
11	HUMOUROUS VARIATIONS on	"Three Blind Mice"	*Lotter*
12	FINALE	"Puppchen"	*Gilbert*

GOD SAVE THE KING.

SPECIAL 3 DAYS' ENGAGEMENT.   H.M. SEAFORTH HIGHLANDERS.

Weston Park, Thursday, Friday & Saturday, July 16th, 17th & 18th,

Two Performances Daily at 3 and 7-30.

THE SHEFFIELD CHORAL UNION ON FRIDAY NIGHT ONLY, AT 7.30.

G. Slater & Son, Printers, 39 Bridge Street, Sheffield.

Weston Park was probably the most important venue for the Music in the Parks seasons arranged by the Bands Sub-Committee and the concerts attracted enormous audiences. Over 60,000 people are said to have attended the final concert in 1902. Although they would not have known it at the time, this concert by the Scots Guards took place just days before the start of the First World War and must have marked the end of an era.

The band of the Hallamshire Battalion, York and Lancaster Regiment, would have been heard regularly in the parks. In addition to the many local brass bands, the concert seasons also featured military bands. Some of the best-known regimental bands, such as the Coldstream Guards and the Royal Marines, visited Sheffield and the Commanding Officers of regiments stationed at Hillsborough Barracks sometimes offered the services of their musicians.

A concert in Weston Park on 23 August 1970 by the City of Sheffield Brass Band. The last full season of band concerts was in 1957 but the Weston Park bandstand remained in use until the early 1980s. Although now sadly neglected, it is the last remaining park bandstand in the city.

The York and Lancaster Regiment War Memorial in Weston Park was unveiled on 7 July 1923 by Field Marshall Lord Plumer. The figure of Victory which stands on the granite column was designed by Francis Jahn and modelled by G.N. Morewood, who was also responsible for the officer at the foot of the memorial. Another craftsman, Roy Smith, produced the figure of the private soldier.

A sombre crowd watches as a wreath is laid at the foot of the York and Lancaster Regiment Memorial on Armistice Day. The regiment lost 8,814 officers and men in the First World War.

The new university buildings viewed from Weston Park. Perhaps the gardeners with their horse and cart have just completed the floral display on the lawn. This incorporates the city's coat of arms and was probably an annual display to honour the current Lord Mayor, as can be seen in the picture below.

The Lord Mayoralty of Alderman J.G. Graves in 1926-27 is recorded in flowers. Graves made an enormous contribution to the development of the city's parks through his gifts of land and this tribute by the gardeners in Weston Park seems particularly appropriate.

The Winter Street entrance to Weston Park. The gateway and the Swiss-style lodge were demolished in the 1950s as part of a land exchange with the university which allowed the construction of the new library. The fate of these gates is unknown but the similar gates on Western Bank were stolen in September 1994 and have never been recovered.

The monument to Ebenezer Elliott was the first statue to be moved to one of the parks. It originally stood in High Street and was re-sited in Weston Park in 1875. The Town Guns standing next to the monument were originally used by the Loyal Independent Sheffield Volunteers. They later became the property of the Town Trustees and were in the care of the Sheffield Artillery Volunteers until 1897 when they were given to the Sheffield Corporation. The Town Guns were put on display in Weston Park in December 1897 but they also appear in photographs taken in other parks.

Weston Park conservatory photographed in 1956. The conservatory and the adjoining formal gardens were one of the city's contributions to mark the Festival of Britain in 1951. Unfortunately it became neglected in later years, proposals to convert it into a restaurant were rejected and eventually a eucalyptus tree could be seen growing through the roof. It was demolished in 1999.

The conservatory displayed a wide variety of decorative plants throughout the year. This photograph was taken in July 1959.

The 'Firth Park March' was played by the Band of the Hallamshire Rifle Volunteers when the Prince of Wales opened the park on 16 April 1875. The 36-acre park was a gift to the town from Mark Firth. It had originally formed part of the larger Page Hall estate, which he bought in 1873.

On 21 August 1875 the magazine *The Graphic* published this illustration of the vast crowds gathered in Firth Park to greet the Prince and Princess of Wales as they arrived in a procession of forty carriages from Victoria Station. This was the first of the great royal visits to Sheffield and triumphal arches were built to decorate the route of the procession. The royal party was the guest of Mark Firth at Oakbrook and during the following day they visited the works of Thos. Firth & Sons, Charles Cammell & Co. and Joseph Rodgers & Sons.

The open spaces of Firth Park are being enjoyed by large numbers of people in this view looking towards Vivian Road. The park was less formal than Weston Park and local newspapers praised the lack of restrictions. Working men, they suggested, would appreciate the facilities if they were not constantly instructed to keep off the grass or reminded of the penalties for damaging flowers or shrubs.

A view of the drinking fountain, lake and pavilion in the 1900s. This was one of the more formal areas of Firth Park and the fountain is the focus of many photographs. Much of the planned work was unfinished at the time of the Prince's visit and Mark Firth spent an additional £9,000 before a second ceremony on 22 August 1876 to mark its completion.

Generations of children must have leaned over these railings to feed the ducks. Only the fashions reveal that this photograph was taken in the 1900s.

Above: After the Second World War the lake in Firth Park was renovated and it became a shallow paddling and boating pool. Members of the Sheffield Ship Model Society were a familiar sight there in the 1950s and in 1953 it was announced that the Society's Chairman, Mr G.H. Wilkin, was making a thirty-five minute film of their activities. The film is not in the city's film archive and we would be pleased to hear from anyone who may know anything about it.

Right: Two young boys look on enviously as the radio-controlled model ships are prepared for sailing on the pond in Firth Park.

The regular Sunday sailing of model boats was obviously a popular attraction for local people. The pond was eventually filled in and became a play area.

The imposing Clock Tower Pavilion at the entrance to Firth Park. The building incorporated a park keeper's house and three refreshment rooms, one giving access to a veranda. It was always a centre for the local community and a few years ago a former resident recalled life there in the 1930s when jugs of tea were served and whist drives and old-time dancing were organised. The building was badly damaged in an arson attack in 1995 but by 1998 it had reopened and was again providing welcome community facilities.

A large audience enjoys a concert at the Firth Park bandstand. This was probably part of the celebrations held to mark the Coronation of King George V in 1911. Royal occasions were marked in great style and although the centrepiece of this occasion was a pageant at Bramall Lane, the parks hosted concerts, firework displays, bonfires and even cinematograph entertainment by the Sheffield Photo Company.

Firth Park from Hucklow Road in 1949, showing the newly constructed entrance. The formal gardens beyond the lodge were also created at this time. There is an interesting range of street furniture on the road outside the park, including an early concrete telephone kiosk, a police call box and a hut possibly being used by the workmen or by transport staff.

In 1886 37 acres of the Meersbrook Park estate were bought from the Lands Allotment Company Ltd for £7,500. Although it was just across the border in Derbyshire, the new park would serve a growing population in south Sheffield. At the meeting of the General Purposes and Parks Committee on 14 September 1887 it was decided that the park should be opened to the public on 17 September and that the formal opening be deferred to an early date. The delay was probably rather longer than intended and the official opening did not take place until September 1987 when the park celebrated its centenary.

The gardeners pause to admire their work in about 1910. Meersbrook Park included two important buildings, Bishop's House and Meersbrook Hall. The hall was built in 1780 for Benjamin Roebuck, a Sheffield banker, and later became one of the residences of the Shore family. They also owned Norton Hall. Rooms in the hall were converted to house the Ruskin Museum, which moved there from Walkley and opened on 15 April 1890.

Officials of the Meersbrook Park Sunday School Union in 1912. The Union held its first gathering in the park on Whit Monday in 1889. Among the Sunday schools taking part in that original meeting were Oak Street Methodist, Trinity Methodist, Heeley Wesleyan and Trinity Methodist Mission.

The Whit Monday gathering in Meersbrook Park in 1912 attracted 10,000 people including 7,000 children and teachers from twenty-two Sunday schools. They marched there in three processions, led by the Imperial Prize Band, St Peter's Concertina Band and the Midland Railway Band. The hymn singing was accompanied by the bandsmen of the Imperial Band.

The Avenue in Meersbrook Park. Although the grounds of the hall had been neglected, they contained a number of original features which were retained when improvements were made. Visitors could stroll along the Avenue in their Sunday-best clothes and enjoy the views across the park and beyond.

The bowling greens, looking towards the top of Meersbrook Park Road. The first green was laid in 1907 but this was not the first bowling green in the area. On 7 October 1874 the Meersbrook Proprietory Bowling Green Club was formed and they bought land in Victoria Road, later renamed Shirebrook Road.

A policeman passes by during construction work in Endcliffe Woods. There were 33 acres of land and a large sum was spent on laying paths and building fences. It all had to be done by hand. The first 24½ acres were bought for £6,108 in 1885 and a further 9 acres were then acquired by the Queen's Jubilee Committee in 1887 and presented to the town to mark the anniversary.

A party of children pose at the stepping stones. This was one of the most popular locations in the park for photographs. Fortunately the water level is low on this occasion or there would have been some wet feet.

The bathing pool in Endcliffe Woods in 1895. There were three dams in the park. One was used for boating, one was stocked with wildfowl and the third, Endcliffe Wheel, became a bathing pool. In 1907 there were complaints about the 'improper use' of bathing sheds and an unclimbable fence was erected to ensure that the pool could be closed at night. Vandalism and the misuse of parks is not new.

The Endcliffe Woods boating pool was obviously popular with the young men of the area. Grinding at Holme Wheel probably ended in the 1880s but the buildings survived and were used as a store. The boat oars can be seen on racks on the wall. In 1896 John Thompson of Rotherham paid £4 for the right to operate the boats with the condition that charges should not exceed 6d per half hour per person.

Serious anglers were not welcome on all the dams but catching tiddlers was accepted. The girls are probably playing at the side of the former Nether Spurgear Wheel in Endcliffe Woods.

The drinking fountain near the entrance to Endcliffe Woods was popular with these children despite the time of year. And the animals had not been forgotten. The elaborate bronze fountain inside the shelter incorporated three drinking goblets on chains but it also supplied a drinking trough for dogs and other animals. The fountain was presented in August 1889 by Mrs W.G. Blake in memory of her late father, Mr Thomas Jessop.

It is a quiet day in on Ecclesall Road. The entrance to the park is marked by the stone pillars on the right of the picture, which were originally the toll bar gate posts, and the refreshment rooms in the park can be seen over the wall to the left of the shelter. The poster is advertising a concert in High Hazels Park by the famous Foden Motor Works Prize Band. The postmark is 1915.

The details on the back of this photograph read simply 'Unemployed – Endcliffe Park'. The group was probably viewed with some suspicion by the park keepers.

The gentleman has stopped to admire Endcliffe Park's latest acquisition (from about 1929 it was being referred to as Endcliffe Park rather than Endcliffe Woods). The statue of Victoria was moved from the top of Fargate on 24 February 1930 to make way for road improvements. It was originally unveiled on 11 May 1905 and had replaced the Jubilee monument, which had already been moved to Endcliffe in 1903. The card is postmarked 10 June 1931.

The Sheffield Show in Endcliffe Park. The show began during the Second World War as the Food Production Show and became the Sheffield Show in 1949. It was changed in 1958 to provide more entertainment, particularly for children, although some traditional features were retained. As the Parks and Burial Grounds Committee reported, 'The Sheffield Transport Band have also given a great deal of pleasure to the middle-aged and elderly people who still enjoy listening to a brass band.'

The Hillsborough Park bandstand prepared for a concert. The postcard was sent in 1909. The park originally formed part of the estate of Hillsborough Hall, which can be seen in the distance. In 1890 Sheffield Corporation bought 50 acres, which at that time lay outside the boundary in the parish of Ecclesfield, from the trustees of the late J. Willis Dixon for £15,000. After improvements had been carried out the park opened on 8 August 1892.

The location of this picture of the Sheffield Police Band is not given but it was possibly taken in Hillsborough Park. The photographer, W.R. Moore, was based on Langsett Road and many of his postcards show scenes on the north-west side of the city. The Police Band was formed in the 1870s and would have attended civic occasions as well as giving concerts in the parks.

The new Hillsborough Library, *c.*1910. When Hillsborough Park first opened the hall and grounds remained private and were leased to one of the former owners. In 1901 boundary extensions brought the park and the surrounding districts into the city and it was proposed that the hall should become a library to serve the rapidly developing area. After some delay two rooms were opened as a branch library in 1906.

One of the bowling greens in Hillsborough Park. The provision of greens in a number of parks encouraged a revival of the game and in 1908 a Parks Bowling Association was formed. Teams from Hillsborough, Meersbrook, Firth Park, High Hazels and Crookesmoor Recreation Ground competed for a new trophy presented by the *Daily Independent* and the first winners, Hillsborough, received the award on 1 October 1908.

HILLSBORO' PARK. SHEFFIE...   G.B&SONS № 429

HILLSBORO' PARK. SHEFFIELD.   G.B&SONS№423.

Above: The boating lake at Hillsborough, *c.* 1905. The original lake was enlarged to make it suitable for boating and the ducks which nested on the islands were an additional attraction for younger visitors. However, some of the local boys were reported to have been more interested in its potential for fishing. Unfortunately when the park opened fishing was prohibited.

Left: The photographer was probably keen to include these children in his picture of the shelter in Hillsborough Park. He obviously took several photographs during this visit as they were published by G. Bagshaw & Sons in a numbered sequence of postcards which included both the pictures on this page.

Opposite, above: The Avenue in Hillsborough Park leading towards Penistone Road, *c.* 1905. Despite the various improvements, the park retained much of the character of an eighteenth-century landscape and the avenue was probably an original feature.

One of the rows of machinery exhibits at the 66th Great Yorkshire Show held at Hillsborough Park in August 1903. This was only the fourth occasion that the show had been held in Sheffield and nearly 55,000 people attended. It returned to Hillsborough in 1923 and was held at Coal Aston in 1935 before being based permanently in Harrogate. There were obviously at least two photographers present but there seem to be few surviving pictures of the event.

High Hazels Park met the need for a park to serve the Attercliffe and Darnall districts. The 47-acre estate was bought from the Duke of Norfolk and the Jeffcocks for £10,875 in 1894 and, after fencing and other improvements, the first portion opened to the public on 6 August 1895. The postcard is from a later period, possibly the 1930s.

High Hazels Museum shown on a postcard sent in 1913. The house was built in 1850 for William Jeffcock and the family lived there until 1864. It was then occupied mainly by tenants, an arrangement which continued when the property was bought by the Corporation. There were various proposals for its use and in December 1901 it opened as a museum with displays of local history. At one point attendances reached 60,000 a year but its popularity declined and it closed shortly after the outbreak of war in 1939. After the war the house became the pavilion for Tinsley Park Golf Course.

DUCK POND, HIGH HAZELS PARK, SHEFFIELD.

The lake was one of the original features in High Hazels and perhaps deserved a more complimentary description than the caption 'duck pond' which appears on this picture. The source of this illustration is rather unusual. It is one of nine combined writing sheets and envelopes with a view which make up *The Tourist's View Writing Pad*.

A speaker addresses the crowd from High Hazels bandstand during the annual May Labour Demonstration on 27 May 1906. The procession had assembled in Brompton Road, Attercliffe and, with no less than six brass bands and many local trade union banners, made its way to the park to hear speeches from labour leaders. The principal guest was Will Crooks MP. The use of the parks on Sundays for demonstrations was controversial and in 1907 the City Council passed a resolution requiring the General Purposes and Parks Committee to refuse any application.

Another event held in High Hazels Park was the annual demonstration of the Darnall Medical Aid Society. The society was formed in 1897 to raise funds to employ a nurse in the Darnall area. Members paid a subscription of a farthing per week but the main source of income was the demonstration. Originally a parade led by local bands made its way to the park where there were speeches and hymn singing, but it gradually became a more elaborate event with decorated wagons, people in fancy dress and, as here, a jazz band and concert party.

The ice cream seller is still a familiar sight outside many park gates. This hand cart is outside the entrance to High Hazels Park, probably in around 1930.

Crookes Recreation Ground looking towards Oxford Street. 450,000 loads of material were used to build the embankment for the new Crookes Valley Road and the slope was laid out with winding paths, steps and shrubberies. The land below, owned by the Water Committee, was rented as a recreation ground.

On the other side of Crookes Valley Road a more formal area was created with a shelter, bowling green and tennis courts. Sheffield's first municipal bowling green was provided at Crookes in 1905. The main path on the left follows the edge of the Old Great Dam and roughly marks the route of the original Great Dam Road which made a steep descent into the valley before the embankment was built.

A poor-quality image but one of the few early photographs showing sporting activities in the parks. Following the success of the bowling green, a tennis court was built at Crookes in 1907.

In 1951 the redundant Old Great Dam was converted into a boating lake and the former recreation ground was renamed Crookes Valley Park. It was officially opened on 5 July as part of Sheffield's contribution to the Festival of Britain. There were thirty rowing dinghies available for hire and in May 1953 a specially built motor launch, the Queen Elizabeth, was added to the fleet. Frank Noble, the Head Keeper with twenty years naval service, was the new 'skipper'. Overlooking the lake was the new Festival Restaurant. According to the Manager of the Civic Restaurants Department, the Dam House Restaurant ('not a café') would serve first class meals of a continental standard.

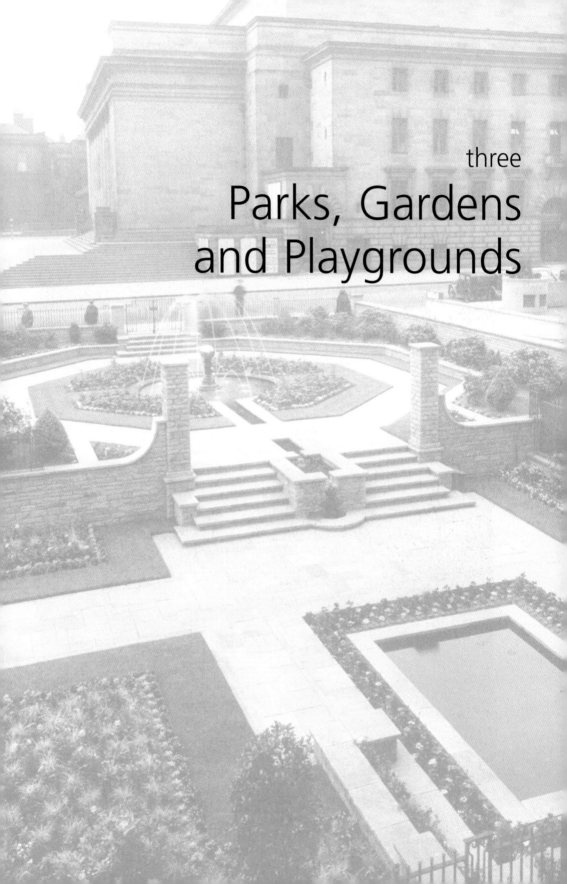

three
Parks, Gardens
and Playgrounds

Enjoying the gardens of Abbeyfield, probably in about 1900 when the house was still a private residence. The house was built in the late eighteenth century for William Pass and was extended and the grounds enlarged by the Wake family in the second half of the nineteenth century. Stone walls surrounded a typical villa garden with over 5 acres of trees, shrubs and lawns as well as ornamental areas and the small lake.

In 1909 Abbeyfield was in the hands of the trustees of the late Reginald Wake and development of the site was being considered. It was an ideal opportunity to create a park in an area with few amenities but the Council rejected the first proposal because the asking price of £10,000 was considered too high. However, when the Town Trustees offered £1,500 towards the cost and H.J. Wilson MP a further £1,000, the Council agreed to find the remainder. The photograph probably dates from about 1930.

According to the caption, this tug-of-war contest is being held as part of a military tournament at Millhouses. The postmark is 1908, indicating that the event must have taken place before Millhouses Park was created. In April 1909 it was announced that a new park was to be formed between the railway line and the road from Millhouses to Beauchief Station. 11½ acres were to be purchased from Earl Fitzwilliam, who donated a further 16 acres.

One of the rustic bridges across the River Sheaf in Millhouses Park. The main railway line is in the background. The postcard was sent to a friend in Lincoln on 21 September 1914 by 'Lottie', who lived at 995 Abbeydale Road, just beyond the junction with Archer Road. She was obviously taking an interest in the local park and asked, 'What do you think to photo. I think that it is a very good one.'

Construction of the open-air swimming pool at Millhouses provided work for about 100 men at a time of mass unemployment. There was obviously a great deal of manual labour, with only the horses and carts to help. The facts about the project were impressive. The pool was 110 yards long and 100 feet across and varied in depth from 3 feet to 9 feet. It held 1.25 million gallons of water and was constantly fed with filtered water drawn from the River Sheaf, ensuring a complete change every thirty-six hours.

HIGH DIVE, MILLHOUSES BATHING POOL. 6381.

Above: The pool opened on 15 August 1929 when an estimated 20,000 people occupied every possible vantage point to watch the displays of swimming, diving and water polo. During the formal proceedings it was announced that after much deliberation the Council had decided to allow mixed bathing. Until then this had been restricted to a few sessions at Glossop Road Baths. The pool was very popular in hot weather but the water could also be very cold and dark. It finally closed in 1967.

Opposite, below: The paddle boats on the pool in Millhouses Park were always very popular. It was also a regular venue for model yacht racing. The pool was on the site of Skargell or Bartin Wheel, the names being those of former owners or tenants of the site. The wheel ceased working in about 1850 and towards the end of the century the dam is described as a skating rink on Ordnance Survey maps. The pool was probably photographed here in the 1960s and it closed in 1996.

Above: There is a very serious discussion taking place among these senior citizens at Millhouses Park. The idea of providing meeting places for 'old and infirm men' began before the First World War and proved to be so popular that by 1936 there were eighteen shelters in parks and recreation grounds. They were equipped with a stove for heating, tables and chairs and, in some cases, even electric light. There were also playing cards, dominoes and draughts.

A packed Millhouses Lido in the 1970s. The new leisure pool which opened in 1970 was unlike anything seen before and the modern hexagonal design quickly won architectural awards. Visitors were expected from all over the city but in the age of the car they would no longer have to rely on public transport. A new car park with 130 spaces was planned as part of the development.

Unlike the old pool, where non-swimmers were refused admission, the lido provided facilities for the whole family. There were shallow pools for the children and spectators could relax and sunbathe on the terraces. The admission charge when it opened was 3s for adults and 1s 6d for children on Sundays and bank holidays and 2s or 1s during the week. It closed for repairs in August 1988 but the closure became permanent and the pools were eventually filled in.

John George Graves (1866-1945). Graves was probably Sheffield's greatest benefactor. He was born in Horncastle, Lincolnshire and after spending some years in Heckmondwike he came to Sheffield in 1880 to be apprenticed to W. Wichman, a watchmaker in Gibraltar Street. Watches were to be the basis of his early business success and he went on to build up a huge enterprise based on mass advertising, mail order and credit payment. At one point he employed 3,000 people on twenty-seven sites in the city. He developed a great affection for Sheffield and his personal gifts, and those of the J.G. Graves Charitable Trust (set up in 1930 to ensure that his work would continue) touched on many aspects of life. They included the Graves Trust Homes, hospitals and health facilities, the Graves Art Gallery together with many pictures from his own collection, and the University Students' Union. However, it was in the provision of parks, playgrounds and sports facilities and the safeguarding of important open spaces that he made the greatest impact.

Norton Hall and Park as it appeared in a brochure for the sale on 2 July 1850. The estate was being sold by Samuel Shore, who had rebuilt the hall and extended the grounds. Later owners included Bernard Alexander Firth who bought the estate in 1902. In 1924 the hall and some of the surrounding land was acquired by the Voluntary Hospitals and it seemed possible that the remaining parts would fall into the hands of developers.

A parasol is needed as these ladies enjoy a boating expedition on the lake at Norton Hall. The photograph is dated 1892. The thatched boathouse stood at the side of the largest of the three lakes in the park

It is a very different winter scene on the same lake as the ice is prepared for skating.

One of the woodland paths in Graves Park in about 1930. By the 1920s the city's suburbs were still expanding and it was recognised that the Norton Hall estate had great potential as a public park. There were level open areas for sports facilities, wooded valleys and walks and three lakes suitable for boating and fishing. Part of the estate was bought by J.G. Graves and presented to the city in October 1925 and further gifts of land took it to over 200 acres, making it the largest park in Sheffield.

The quarry in Cobnar Woods which was once used as the Norton rifle range. In 1927 it was proposed that the quarry should become an open-air auditorium. It was said that a lady, well known in Sheffield music circles, had come across the quarry while strolling through the park and had immediately realised its potential. The suggestion was adopted by the Parks Committee and preparations were made for a summer opening.

A park keeper is ensuring that the grass at the Bolehill Lodge entrance to Graves Park is kept neat and tidy. Beyond the gates, there is no evidence of any housing development on Derbyshire Lane.

BOWLING GREEN & TENNIS COURTS, GRAVES PARK

Above: The Graves Park bowling green and tennis courts adjacent to Charles Ashmore Road, probably in the 1950s.

Opposite below: Members of the Sheffield Musical Union performing in the open-air theatre. In 1928 the Music in the Parks programme introduced a series of evening concerts in Graves Park which included bands, choral societies and concert groups. The Committee aimed to encourage local talent and some of the performers included the Victoria Hall Choral Society, the Lilias Hanson Pantomime Party, Sheffield Recreation Concertina Band and the Sheffield Orpheus Choir.

Left: Graves Park has always been an ideal location for cross-country races. The Universities Athletic Union championships were held in Sheffield on 20 February 1938 but local supporters were disappointed. Sheffield University's G.S. Burdett was beaten by a competitor from London University.

Below: The café and rose garden is still one of the most popular features of Graves Park. The refreshment pavilion dates from 1927 when it was built alongside Dower House, reputed to be even older than Norton Hall itself. The formal garden in front of the pavilion was designed in 1938 by E.O. Sadler, who had also designed Beauchief Garden. It featured rose beds separated by a geometrical pattern of paving, with stone walls and steps and a pergola. A statue of Peter Pan originally stood in the centre.

A Whitsuntide gathering in Graves Park in the 1930s includes a contingent from Woodseats Wesleyan Methodist Church. The crowd is gathered near the Cobnar Road entrance. This piece of land was bought by J.G. Graves in about 1931 and it provided an additional entrance to the park and an area which became the children's playground.

The plant nurseries at Graves Park were built on the site of the former kitchen garden of Norton Hall. A nursery was first established in 1921 and, although the land was bought by J.G. Graves in 1936, tenants remained until 1939. One of the tenants was H.D. Widdowson & Son who, apart from growing fruit, flowers and vegetables, bred the Chantreyland viola. After the war the nurseries were expanded by the Council and eventually became the Recreation Department's main plant centre. They closed in 1999.

The next donation made by J.G. Graves was on the other side of the city at Shiregreen. 112 acres were bought in 1929 and the new park, named Concord at the suggestion of Graves, opened in September 1930. This view towards the main entrance on Shiregreen Lane gives a glimpse of the ornate wrought-iron gates erected in 1932. They came from Hayes Park in Kent, originally the home of William Pitt, and were brought to Sheffield by Charles Boot.

Gardeners at work in Concord Park. There are surprisingly few pictures of the staff who maintained the parks and gardens and these men certainly had enough work to occupy their time. A further 37 acres were added to Concord in 1932, making it the second largest park, and according to a later booklet there were two bowling greens, ten tennis courts, twenty-three football pitches, seven cricket pitches, a nine-hole golf course, a miniature golf course and a putting green.

Furnace Hill Playground, opened in October 1933. Many people lived in areas which lacked open spaces and recreational facilities and the street or court was the traditional playground. Slum clearance schemes created new sites, often still surrounded by derelict buildings or factories, which were used to build playgrounds for children who lived too far from the parks.

Some of the local children are eagerly awaiting the completion of Matthew Street Playground at Shalesmoor. Most of the equipment is in place but there seems to be room for three more roundabouts. The driving force behind the scheme to build playgrounds was again J.G. Graves but there were also contributions from other benefactors. The cost of the sites was nominal but equipping them and providing a shelter and toilets was more expensive. The figure for Matthew Street is not available but Crown Alley Playground cost £989 1s 1d to equip.

Above: The equipment would not meet modern health and safety standards but the white lines do indicate the 'danger' areas in front of the swings. The equipment at Bacon Lane Playground included two merry-go-rounds, two joy wheels, one plank swing, two rocking horses, two whirling platforms, three swings and one ocean wave.

The Lord Mayor, Alderman Ernest Wilson, addresses a very orderly audience at the opening of Surrey Road Playground in May 1933. This was in contrast to the experience at the opening at Matthew Street. So many children had gathered that the official party was unable to reach the playground, the gates had to be opened to relieve the pressure of the crowd and the formal ceremony had to be abandoned.

Beauchief Garden was created on land adjoining the dam of Abbeydale Works which was bought by the J.G. Graves Charitable Trust in 1935. While the future of the works as an industrial museum was being decided, E.O. Sadler, Manager of the Parks Department, designed the new garden, making full use of the stream which fed the dam. He also used paving salvaged from slum clearance houses to construct the paths. The work was completed in 1936.

Opposite below: When the playgrounds had been laid out and equipped, they were handed over to the Council, who provided a keeper and carried out maintenance work. This 'Parkie' at Furnace Hill would have worked a forty-seven-hour week and was paid around £2 10s 6d, depending on benefits such as housing and fuel. Furnace Hill Playground was provided by the trustees of the late T.W. Ward.

The City Hall Garden was formally opened by the Lord Mayor, Alderman Mrs A.E. Longden, on 3 August 1937. It was another gift from J.G. Graves, who explained that his main aim in creating a garden was to prevent any further development and thus preserve the setting of the City Hall. The owners of the Grand Hotel must also have been delighted with the removal of the hoardings which had surrounded the site next to the hotel entrance. The City Hall's famous Saturday dances are being advertised with music by Bernard Taylor and his band.

The main feature of the garden was an ornamental fountain with sixteen jets of water which sprayed onto a stainless steel globe. It was set in the centre of an octagonal paved area with flowerbeds and grass plots. Unlike other gardens, the public did not normally have access. The photograph was taken in the 1940s when one of the neighbouring cinemas was experiencing an identity crisis. The Regent became the Gaumont on 27 July 1946 and both names are being displayed.

Longley Park in 1947 looking towards Crowder Road and Longley Lane. Beyond the swimming pool are the tennis courts, the bowling green and the pavilion. In 1926 over 50 acres were transferred to the Parks Committee in order to create a park to serve the new housing estates. The picture shows the area in transition. Some of the council houses can be seen behind the trees on the right but the old buildings of Longley Hall are still standing in the background.

Longley Park Swimming Pool was a gift to the city by Mr G.H. Lawrence, a cutlery and razor-blade manufacturer. He also donated the open-air pool in Hathersage. According to the newspaper reports, 'The rain was beating on the water in the pool' when the official opening took place on Saturday 3 September 1938, but at least the water would be warm. It was Sheffield's first heated open-air pool. There was also a glazed sunbathing pavilion for when the weather improved.

Five intrepid swimmers at Longley. During the first year 14,582 people collected the paper sack for their clothes and made their way to one of the dressing cabins before taking the plunge.

Two divers have been caught in flight as they take off from the five-metre board. The pool was in a small valley and the slopes provided good vantage points for the spectators. Nearby there was a paddling pool and sandpit to occupy the children.

Above: The story of the Peace Gardens begins with the closure and demolition of St Paul's Church. The population of the city centre parishes had declined and despite its architectural importance St Paul's was closed on 12 December 1937. The site was bought by the City Council and demolition of the church quickly followed between March and May 1938.

St Paul's Garden in 1943, looking towards Norfolk Street. Although Alderman Rowlinson's suggestion was apparently never officially adopted, the site was laid out as a garden. Paths surrounded a central octagonal area and the rows of seats made it a popular city centre resting place.

The garden became very popular with the public and many people will remember it as it appears here in 1969 before the construction of the Town Hall extension. The garden has matured but the original design survives. Although it was popularly known as the Peace Gardens, it was still officially St Paul's Garden. It remained so until 8 May 1985 when the Lord Mayor unveiled a plaque renaming the garden.

Opposite below: Clearing St Paul's graveyard in 1938. The remains were reburied at Abbey Lane Cemetery. The Council's main motive in buying the land was to safeguard the site for possible development as municipal offices but other suggestions made at the time included an ice rink and a combined underground car park and air-raid shelter. Meanwhile, Neville Chamberlain had returned from Munich and one of the proposals made to mark the event came from the Lord Mayor, Ernest Rowlinson. During a speech in October 1938 he proposed that the site of St Paul's should be 'a restful, pleasant open space'.

The Lord Mayor, Alderman Fred Marshall, and J.G. Graves enjoy an impromptu game at the opening of Richmond Sports Park on 8 October 1934. The land was a gift from the J.G. Graves Charitable Trust, who also gave £500 towards the cost of laying out the sports facilities.

A fancy dress competition at a Gloops Gala in Hollinsend Recreation Ground in the 1950s. Gloops was the *Telegraph and Star*'s famous cartoon cat who first appeared in March 1926. In 1928 the Gloops Club was formed and in its heyday it organised activities for thousands of children. Hollinsend was one of a number of recreation grounds where the emphasis was on the provision of sports and play facilities for the neighbouring housing estates. In south-east Sheffield, where mining was one of the traditional industries, the Miners' Welfare Committee contributed to the purchase of several recreation grounds.

four

Woodlands and Open Spaces

Despite their Sunday-best clothes, the members of Oughtibridge Church have used the backdrop of Wharncliffe Crags to create a group photograph with a difference. The date is around 1914. The Crags were a favourite destination for excursions and as early as 1836 John Holland, writing in the *Sheffield Mercury*, said: 'Although summer is the chief season when visitors, especially ladies, may be expected to ramble – if not, indeed, actually to scramble – among these rocks with pleasure there is no part of the year, mid-winter scarcely excepted, at which Wharncliffe does not present appropriate and striking beauties to the observation of those who, having health and strength for the task, will be at the trouble of climbing up the hill to look at them.'

This well-dressed gentleman has abandoned his tripod and equipment to admire the view from Table Rock on Wharncliffe Crags. The land was owned by Earl Fitzwilliam but it was open to the public on Mondays, Wednesdays and Saturdays.

J.W. Puttrell and W.J. Watson climbing the Great Chimney on Wharncliffe Crags in 1902. Puttrell was a pioneer rock climber and cave explorer and much of his early climbing was done at Wharncliffe. One of the climbs on the Crags, Puttrell's Progress, is named after him.

These men are taking advantage of the seats installed in Great Roe Wood at Pitsmoor as part of its conversion to pleasure grounds. In 1897 a deputation of local councillors approached the Duke of Norfolk with a proposal to open the wood as a public park. The Duke agreed to donate 20 acres to commemorate the Diamond Jubilee and the Queen's visit but one suggestion, that it should be known as Victoria Park, was never adopted.

An afternoon stroll in Whiteley Woods. This 'Real Photograph' card from Boots Cash Chemists was posted in 1915. Land in the Porter Valley beyond Endcliffe Woods was acquired in several stages. In 1896 the first two plots, totalling over 41 acres and including four dams, were purchased for £6,100. Along with Endcliffe Woods, this provided a narrow but continuous walk of about two miles along the valley to Forge Houses.

Having left Endcliffe Woods, the entrance to Whiteley Woods from Rustlings Road marked the beginning of the next stage of the walk along the Porter Valley. The Park Superintendent's lodge dates from about 1909. In 1911 Colonel Sir John Bingham presented a further 11 acres to the city which led to the development of Bingham Park.

A postcard from about 1907 shows the footpath past Shepherd Wheel and distant views towards Ranmoor. When the land was first acquired as a park there were still a number of active works along the river and their remains serve as a reminder of how industry has helped shape the landscape. Shepherd Wheel, named after Edward Shepherd who leased the site around 1749, is one of the oldest recorded sites. The earliest possible reference is to a will proved in 1566.

Until about 1900 these farm buildings, called Porter House on the Ordnance Survey maps, stood on the land opposite Shepherd Wheel.

Grinders at work at Shepherd Wheel. When commercial working ceased in about 1930 Shepherd Wheel was maintained by the Society for the Preservation of Old Sheffield Tools and Machinery. Occasional working demonstrations were held until 1941 but the buildings and machinery were then neglected and by 1957 demolition was being considered. It was saved through the efforts of the Council for the Conservation of Sheffield Antiquities who persuaded the City Council to restore the buildings. By 1962 it was again in working order and in the care of Sheffield City Museums.

The photographers themselves have become the subject in this postcard of Ivy Cottages below Wire Mill Dam dating from around 1905. The picturesque cottages were another popular subject for photographers and postcard publishers. The area was known as Bowser Bottom.

The unveiling of the Thomas Boulsover Memorial at Wire Mill Dam on 15 April 1929. Boulsover, the famous inventor of Sheffield Plate, bought the nearby Whiteley Wood Hall and in the 1760s developed Whiteley Wood Rolling Mill on this site. One of the original arches from a window in the mill is said to have been incorporated in the memorial. The memorial was erected thanks to Mr David Flather and unveiled by the Master Cutler, Mr T.G. Sorby.

Left: Walking through Whiteley Woods it is easy to forget how close some of the built-up areas have come to the valley floor. This view of Forge Dam from the hillside shows Brook House and some of the early development on Brookhouse Hill, with Christ Church, Fulwood in the distance.

Below: The buildings of Whiteley Wood Forge were already in use as refreshment rooms in the 1900s. It is said that the present popular café at Forge Dam, now much modified, was originally a wooden chapel building brought from Walkley in 1932.

10.   REFRESHMENT ROOMS, WHITELEY WOODS, SHEFFIELD.

Rowing boats on Forge Dam. John Hutton was probably the last owner of a working forge at Whiteley Wood but by the end of the nineteenth century the dam had become a fishing and boating pool. *Kelly's Directory of Sheffield and Rotherham* for 1893 lists a Herbert Maxfield, farmer and pleasure boat owner, of Forge House, Fulwood.

Straw hats were essential headwear for boating. Although Forge Dam was open to the public for boating and fishing for many years, it did not come into public ownership until 1938. The purchase and subsequent donation of Old May House Farm and Forge Dam by the J.G. Graves Charitable Trust completed the acquisition of the Mayfield Valley and realized the aim of protecting the green belt along the length of the Porter Brook.

A solitary angler. The location of this photograph is unknown but both Wire Mill Dam and Forge Dam were popular spots for fishermen.

Skating in Whiteley Woods. On 6 January 1908 the *Sheffield Daily Independent* reported that there was good ice in many places in the area. Popular spots included Old Forge Dam, the dams in Endcliffe and Whiteley Woods, Wardsend, Butterthwaite Dam at Ecclesfield and the lake in Renishaw Park where the Sheffield Skating Club had its headquarters. The paper also reported a number of tragic accidents on the ice, fortunately none of them in Sheffield.

The entrance to Shirtcliffe Wood at Shubert Bridge in about 1910. Part of the wood was opened as pleasure grounds for the people of Woodhouse in 1898 to mark the Queen's Jubilee.

Children pose by a bridge in Shirtcliffe Wood in another of the series of postcards produced by Jabez Good, a local Woodhouse shopkeeper and photographer.

Two gentlemen have found the perfect spot for quiet relaxation – a rock in the middle of the river. As early as 1899 the Council took the far-sighted decision 'to acquire control of the Rivelin Valley with a view to its preservation for the enjoyment and recreation of the inhabitants of Sheffield'. Further land was acquired as part of the scheme to build a road from Malin Bridge to Hollow Meadows, completed in 1908, but Parliamentary criticism of the scheme almost forced the Water Committee to sell the property. Fortunately Parliament eventually approved the purchase and, despite later proposals to develop the area for housing, the land was safeguarded.

Holme Head Wheel in the Rivelin Valley. The low water level almost makes the stepping stones unnecessary. Holme Head was one of twenty mills along a three-mile stretch of the Rivelin above Malin Bridge. All but two of the mills were originally owned by the Duke of Norfolk but most passed into the hands of the Sheffield Water Company and, in turn, to Sheffield Corporation.

Rowing boats and swings at Upper Cut Wheel. The wheel continued to be leased until 1921, although it was probably not worked in later years. The proprietor of the pleasure grounds may have been David Watson, whose address is given in the 1916 directory as the Tea and Refreshment Rooms, Rivelin Glen.

The Rivelin Valley Bathing Pool, converted from New Dam (which had held water for Spooner Wheel), opened on 18 September 1909. This was rather late in the season as the pool was due to close for the winter at the end of October and only 287 bathers made use of the facilities. Attendance was much better the following year when there were 19,098 bathers. The pool was divided into two sections, for men and boys, but the reports of the Baths Department indicate that ladies were admitted. There was also a large dressing shed and it has been suggested that the pool closed in the late 1930s following a fire which destroyed the building.

Boys 'skinny dipping' in the river. Of course such behaviour would not have been tolerated at the nearby swimming pool. The new byelaws for the management, use and regulation of the open-air bathing pools, approved in 1913, required that 'every bather shall wear proper and sufficient bathing drawers, costume or bathing dress, and such drawers, costume, or dress shall be made of a material that will not discolour the water.'

The streams had always been an unofficial playground for children and, following the success of the paddling stream in Millhouses Park, a similar, larger play area was created at Rivelin. This was another of the schemes prepared for the Festival of Britain and the newspapers reported that even as the Lord Mayor spoke at the official opening on 27 July 1951 the children were already splashing in the water.

The whole family could enjoy a visit to the playground which was constructed next to the Rivelin Paddling Stream. This photograph was taken in August 1953.

Fishing on one of the dams in the Rivelin Valley. At one point in the early 1960s only two dams remained open for fishing because of silting. With an estimated 30,000 anglers in Sheffield, there was a great demand for improved facilities and several dams were dredged as part of a redevelopment scheme. It was claimed that sixteen varieties of fish could be found in the valley.

The winter conditions mean that fishing has given way to a game of football on a snow-covered Wolf Dam.

The newly opened Wyming Brook Drive in about 1910. 210 acres were purchased by the Water Committee in 1906 for £3,589. The main purpose was to prevent pollution in the catchment areas but they also recognised its amenity value and proposed the building of two new roads to open up views of the area. Construction of the roads between Redmires Road and Manchester Road during the winter of 1908/09 provided work for 170 men for three days per week as part of the relief works to combat unemployment. Later views show how the slopes left bare by the construction work were quickly covered by trees and shrubs.

The Rivelin Dams bus outside the Norfolk Arms in 1929. The service from Leopold Street to the Norfolk Arms via Broomhill and Crosspool started on 8 April 1926. There was an hourly bus and the fare to the terminus was 5d. Wyming Brook was also served by the Lodge Moor service which was extended on fine weekends from April 1924.

James Howard and his wife outside their refreshment cabin at Wyming Brook. The bus service to the Norfolk Arms brought more visitors to the area and James Howard started his business by setting up an ice cream stall. When the family owned this cabin, with a shop and living accommodation, they were able to stay on the site during the summer.

The growing number of visitors also provided a useful source of income for local people. Wyming Brook Farm on Redmires Road provided teas and refreshments during the season.

60 WEEKEND

1.15 Comedy sequel, starring Richard
Dreyfuss. See Film Guide; National
Lottery Update; Weatherview. *218200*

2.05 **Natural World** (R)(BSL) *9663427*

2.35 **Indian Food Made Easy**
(R)(AD)(BSL) *9016866*

3.05 **Gardeners' World Top Tips**
(R)(BSL) *1099205*

3.50–6.00 BBC News *72736972*

10.30 Newsnig

11.20 Darts: BD
Highlights
second-ro
at the Lak
Frimley Gre
Tony Green

12.10 Darts Extra *83*

2.10–3.50 BBC News *9*

the life of the c... Last in series.

11.30 London's Fashion Spectacular
12midnight News and Weather **12.30** Book of the Week: And Did Those Feet: Walking Through 2000 Years of British and Irish History. **12.48** Shipping Forecast. **1.00** World Service. **5.20** Shipping Forecast.

Angels By Jim Eldridge. A clash over the teaching of creationism in a school.

3.00 Home Planet
3.30 Scottish Shorts
3.45 Dear Darwin
4.00 Word of Mouth
4.30 Great Lives Bette Davis.
5.00 PM 5.54 (LW) Shipping Forecast. 5.57 Weather.

These children seem to give Fox Glen a special atmosphere. The Clough, renamed Fox Glen, was presented to the people of Stocksbridge by the trustees of the late Samuel Fox in 1911 to commemorate the Coronation of King George V and Queen Elizabeth. Its swimming pool, paddling pools and swings made it an attractive playground for local children.

On 16 August 1919 Stocksbridge Urban District Council gave a civic reception for soldiers and sailors who had served in the war. After a 'substantial tea', the Stocksbridge Brass Band led a procession to Fox Glen where there was an open-air concert and entertainment.

Left: The Wilson family outside their cottage in Bowden Housesteads Wood in about 1890. John Wilson and his son Frank were woodmen employed by the Duke of Norfolk. Their skills would have been required to maintain the coppiced woodlands but by the end of the nineteenth century this tradition had almost disappeared. Bowden Housesteads was one of the woods where new broadleaf trees and conifers were planted for timber production. In 1914 the duke sold 101½ acres to the city for £6,000.

Below: Construction work in progress on the site of the open-air swimming pool at Bowden Housesteads Wood in 1926. The pool was one of the projects undertaken by the Council's General Purposes and Parks Committee to provide work for the unemployed. Most of the labourers on this site were out of work miners.

The pool at Bowden Housesteads probably never looked very appealing. The fence surrounding it was built from railway sleepers and the water had a reputation for being very cold. The pool is still mentioned in the annual report of the Parks Committee for 1938/39 but it probably closed soon after.

The signpost indicates the footpath to Dore across the open spaces of Blacka Moor. The 448 acres of Blacka Plantation and Blacka Hill Moor was among the lots offered for sale by the Duke of Rutland at an auction held at the Royal Victoria Hotel on 5 July 1927. Its purchase by the J.G. Graves Charitable Trust and subsequent presentation to the city prevented any development and ensured that it would remain accessible.

Left: The gravestone of George Yardley, a wood collier, in Ecclesall Woods is a reminder of the importance of charcoal burning, one of the traditional woodland industries. Charcoal was an essential fuel for iron smelting and, later, in making blister steel in cementation furnaces.

Below: Abbey Lane as it passes through Ecclesall Woods. Originally this was the only road through the woods, but in 1921 construction of Whirlowdale Road was approved as one of the schemes to provide work for the unemployed.

Right: Ecclesall Woods was officially opened as a public open space by Princess Mary on 23 August 1928. In 1927 the woods had been in danger of falling into the hands of speculative builders and the 306-acre estate was bought from Earl Fitzwilliam for £45,000. A contribution of £10,000 was given by J.G. Graves and a further £10,000 by the Town Trustees.

Below: Members of the YMCA at camp at Ryecroft Glen. The young men may have been introduced to the pleasures of the 'simple life' under canvas but they obviously enjoyed some home comforts. The tea is poured from a proper teapot and, while some of the campers have to improvise with unturned boxes, others have brought along their chairs. The annual camp was set up for three months over the summer and members paid 2s 6s per week for the use of the tents and equipment. The 1907 season closed with a garden party organised by the ladies of the Social Committee. There were sports and games, refreshments and entertainment provided by the Society's Bijou Orchestra and the Willard Concert Party.

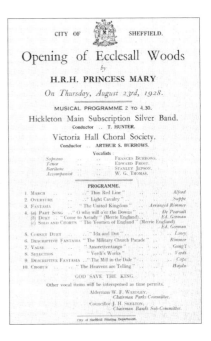

CITY OF   SHEFFIELD.

Opening of Ecclesall Woods
by
H.R.H. PRINCESS MARY
On Thursday, August 23rd, 1928.

MUSICAL PROGRAMME 2 TO 4.30.

Hickleton Main Subscription Silver Band.
Conductor .. T. HUNTER.

Victoria Hall Choral Society.
Conductor .. ARTHUR S. BURROWS.

Vocalists
Soprano	..	FRANCES BURROWS.
Tenor	..	EDWARD FROST.
Baritone	..	STANLEY JEPSON.
Accompanist	..	W. G. THOMAS.

PROGRAMME.

1. MARCH .. .. "Thin Red Line" .. .. *Alford*
2. OVERTURE .. "Light Cavalry" .. *Suppé*
3. FANTASIA .. "The United Kingdom" .. *Arranged Rimmer*
4. (a) PART SONG .. "O who will o'er the Downs" .. *De Pearsall*
 (b) DUET .. "Come to Arcady" (Merrie England) .. *Ed. German*
 (c) SOLO AND CHORUS .. "The Yeomen of England" (Merrie England) .. *Ed. German*
5. CORNET DUET .. .. "Ida and Dot" .. .. .. *Losey*
6. DESCRIPTIVE FANTASIA "The Military Church Parade" .. *Rimmer*
7. VALSE .. .. "Amorettentango" .. .. *Gong'l*
8. SELECTION .. .. "Verdi's Works" .. .. *Verdi*
9. DESCRIPTIVE FANTASIA .."The Mill in the Dale" .. .. *Cope*
10. CHORUS .. .. "The Heavens are Telling" .. *Haydn*

GOD SAVE THE KING.

Other vocal items will be interspersed as time permits.

Alderman W. F. WARDLEY,
Chairman Parks Committee.

Councillor J. H. SKELTON,
Chairman Baths Sub-Committee.

City of Sheffield Printing Department.

A family in the grounds of Beauchief Abbey in 1906. In 1923 the Beauchief Abbey estate was bought by Mr Frank Crawshaw. He developed some of the estate for housing but also showed an appreciation of the area's historic importance by encouraging archaeological investigations. Purchase of land surrounding the abbey by the City Council in 1931 was controversial but at the same time Councillor Crawshaw donated the abbey, cottages and adjoining land on condition that church services would continue.

The seventeenth hole of Beauchief Municipal Golf Course looking towards the abbey, as it appeared in the official handbook published in 1930. In 1914 land at Tinsley Park Wood was purchased by the Council for use as a golf course and this was followed in 1924 by the course at Beauchief. It had originally been a private course leased to the Abbeydale Golf Club and it was acquired by Frank Crawshaw along with the rest of the Beauchief estate. It was initially leased by the Council but in 1931 it was bought, along with woodland stretching from Bocking Lane to Twentywell Lane, for £30,000. The cost of a round was 1s 3d Monday-Friday and 1s 6d on Saturdays and bank holidays.

five

Wartime Parks

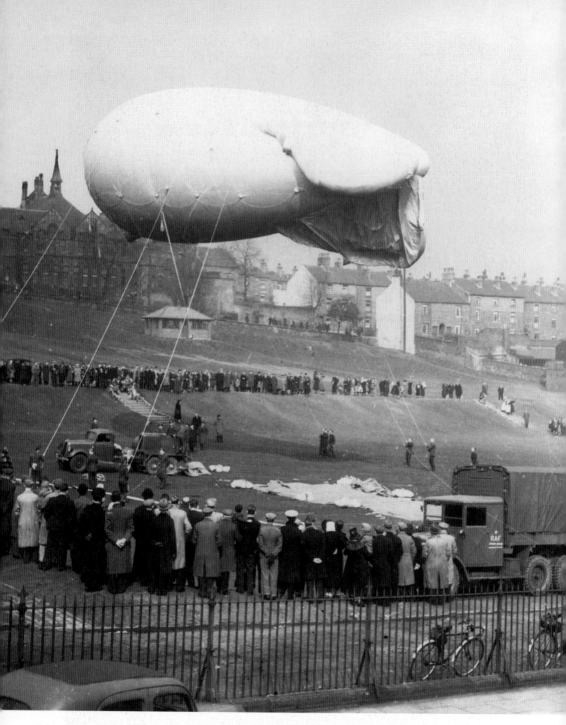

A large crowd has gathered to watch an RAF barrage balloon crew in action on Crookesmoor Recreation Ground in 1939/40. About 1,000 men from the Sheffield area were mobilised in the summer of 1939 to form the three squadrons which made up the Sheffield Balloon Barrage but they were handicapped by a lack of suitable training areas. Work on the RAF station at Norton only began in June 1939 and this crew is probably taking advantage of the open spaces of the recreation ground to practice their new skills.

The Parks Department's Food Production Team in 1941. Although suggestions that vegetables should be grown in the parks instead of flowers were rejected, glasshouses and the nursery grounds were devoted to the growing of food crops. By 1943 140 acres of parkland and sports grounds had been ploughed and a further 200 acres were let to farmers for grazing sheep and cattle. Most of the work on the land in parks was done by the team of youths and Land Army girls.

Harvesting the potato crop in 1943. In that year the Department's food production included 128 tons of potatoes and also 2,085 lbs of beetroot, 2,673lbs of beans, 5,654lbs of cabbages, 1,500lbs of sprouts, 6,877 lettuces, 919lbs of parsnips, 6,732lbs of tomatoes, 19 tons of savoys and 11 tons of swedes.

CITY OF
SHEFFIELD

PARKS
DEPARTMENT

SUMMER HOLIDAYS, 1942

HOLIDAYS ...AT
HOME
PROGRAMME

•

His Majesty's Government expects you to spend your
holiday in and around Sheffield.

Do not travel, or even attempt to travel.

At the request of the Lord Mayor, representatives of
various local organisations have co-operated in the formation
of this programme. Their response has been generous.

In this programme you should be able to find something
of interest for some few days of your holiday.

Members of His Majesty's Forces will be specially welcome
at all shows and events.

You should visit the lovely countryside in the immediate
vicinity of your City.

Visit your Parks, Gardens, Woodlands and Moorlands.

If you have a copy of last year's pamphlet, "Summer
Holidays, 1941" issued by the Parks Department, refer
to it again.

Use the excellent tram service which is available.

There should be no litter. Waste paper is Salvage. It
is a War Weapon.

Enjoy yourselves!

■ ■
■ ■

E. O. SADLER, P.A.S.I., F.R.H.S.
Parks Manager
125 Norfolk Street, Sheffield, 1

● The following programme is subject to
modification. The weekly "Holiday
Programme" will be published in the
local newspapers every Saturday during
the season.

Left: The programme for the 1942 Holidays at Home. The intention is clear: 'His Majesty's Government expects you to spend your holiday in and around Sheffield.' After the fall of France in 1940, war production was increased enormously but only at the expense of high levels of illness and fatigue among the workforce. There were also the added problems caused by the air raids against Britain's cities. Sheffield was attacked in December 1940. The government recognised the importance of an annual holiday but they announced that no special travel arangements would be made. To encourage people to remain at home, local authorities were requested to provide more entertainment and recreation for workers. Sheffield's response was to expand its established Music in the Parks programme and the first Holidays at Home season was staged in 1941. The programme organised by Sheffield was praised as being one of the best in the country. It included concerts, sports, variety shows, open-air dancing and fairgrounds and by 1944 there were over 500 sperate events. 'Enjoy yourselves'.

Left: The Lord Mayor, Alderman H.E. Bridgwater, addresses the crowd from one of the park bandstands during the 1943 Holidays at Home season.

Opposite, above: The formalities over, Alderman Bridgwater tries his luck at the coconut shy. His audience includes a number of balaclava-clad boys who no doubt thought that they could do much better than the Lord Mayor.

Opposite, below: The family seem to be enjoying their outing in this typical fairground scene of sideshows and rides. This fair was probably in Hillsborough Park but in 1943 fun fairs were also held at Concord and Endcliffe.

A large audience is entertained at the Great Variety Show in High Hazels Park in August 1943. The programme included The Great Alzana, King of the High Wire; Ann Yeaman's Football Dogs; the Whitneys, comedy acrobats; Clown Lotto and Constance, trick and comedy cyclists; Raglus, the world's greatest bounce-ball juggler; and Erne Warsaw, a one-man band. There was also a crazy cycle competition with an invitation to try to ride one of the bikes. And all for an admission price of 6d, children 3d.

A battle of wits on the open-air draughts board. The Sheffield Draughts Association provided a board in Millhouses Park in 1933 and players were charged 1d per person per half hour. However, Millhouses does not appear to be the venue for this game in 1943.

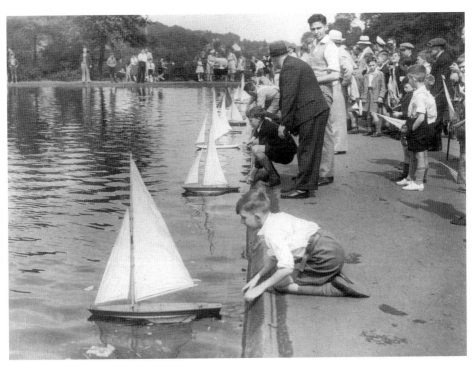

Model yacht racing at Millhouses Park in 1943. There were junior and senior classes in the
Saturday afternoon races so everyone got a chance.

The game of bowls requires concentration. The 1943 Holidays at Home programme included
bowls competitions in Hillsborough Park. Other parks hosted charity cricket matches, five-a-side
football, golf tournaments and swimming galas.

The Punch and Judy show in Meersbrook Park has attracted a large and enthusiastic audience on a July evening in 1942. Although the programme does not give any details, a note on the back of the photograph suggests that the show was given by Professor De Lyle. This was the stage name adopted by George Fox who was a well-known entertainer until his death in 1948.

Forge Dam has always been a place to relax, as this serviceman discovered in 1943.

Merrie England performed at the open-air theatre in Graves Park as part of the 1944 Holidays at Home season. With a cast of over 200 this was the most ambitious event in the programme and it involved a number of well-known names from the local music and drama scene. The producer was Laurie Lingard, the musical director H.E. Taylor and the dances were arranged by Constance Grant.

A gymkhana event at the Food Production Show in Endcliffe Park. The success of the Dig for Victory exhibition at the Graves Art Gallery in 1942 encouraged the Parks Committee to organise a larger outdoor event the following year. The three-day show held in September 1943 featured vegetables, fruit and flowers, rabbits and poultry, beekeeping and a horse show and gymkhana. Despite appalling weather the show attracted over 7,000 people and it became an established event in the parks calendar.

The VE Day thanksgiving service in Weston Park on Sunday 13 May 1945. Nearly 5,000 members of the forces, Civil Defence and other organisations marched from the Town Hall to the park for a service led by the Bishop of Sheffield. Earlier in the day there had been a civic service in the cathedral and in the evening the public were invited to a service in the City Hall.

Opposite: Relaxing in the summer of 1943. The Holidays at Home scheme had been a great success but in 1945, with people looking forward to the end of the war, the programme was renamed 'Summer Entertainment' and it became the model for post-war activities in the parks.

Other local titles published by Tempus

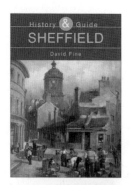

Sheffield History and Guide
DAVID FINE

This highly readable account of Sheffield's past considers the impact of the vast steel-rolling mills, compares the lives of mill owner and mill worker, and looks at life in the countless back-to-backs once strewn across this richly varied city. Using a wealth of photographs, maps and prints, David Fine brings the story up to date and considers what the future may hold for Sheffield.

0-7524-2953-1

Crosspool
JUDITH HANSON

With the expansion of Sheffield over the nineteenth and twentieth centuries, Crosspool has grown from a sparsely-populated backwater into the popular residential area it is today. This collection of over 200 old photographs and postcards illustrates all aspects of life in Crosspool, from work to leisure, homes to commerce and, most importantly, the people who have made the area what it is.

0-7524-2821-7

Around Hackenthorpe
LEONARD WIDDOWSON

This intriguing selection of over 200 archive images recalls the history of Hackenthorpe and the surrounding villages of Moorhole, Owlthorpe, Sothall, Frecheville and Birley Vale over the last century. Accompanied by supporting text, this book is sure to reawaken memories of sporting events, streets, farms, schools and local people in this part of South Yorkshire.

0-7524-3061-0

Sheffield Cinemas
CLIFFORD SHAW FOR SHEFFIELD CINEMA SOCIETY

The first purpose-built cinema in Sheffield was the Picture Palace in Union Street, which opened in 1910. By the outbreak of war in 1914, there were thirty cinemas either completed or under construction. Cinemas suffered a slump during the 1920s but were revived by the advent of the 'talkies' in 1929/30. This pictorial compilation places on record some of the history of local cinemas; hopefully it will be a reminder of what once was.

0-7524-2293-6

If you are interested in purchasing other books published by Tempus, or in case you have difficulty finding any Tempus books in your local bookshop, you can also place orders directly through our website

www.tempus-publishing.com